21st
Century
Skills Library

POWER UP!

BIO-FUELS

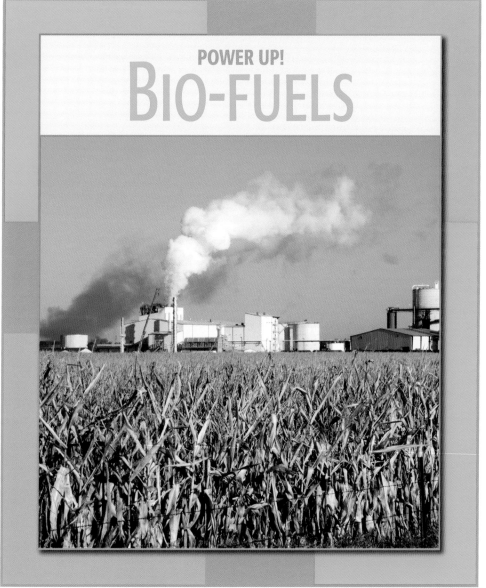

Frank Muschal

Cherry Lake Publishing
Ann Arbor, Michigan

Published in the United States of America by Cherry Lake Publishing
Ann Arbor, MI
www.cherrylakepublishing.com

Photo Credits: Page 10, Photo Courtesy of Library of Congress

Library of Congress Cataloging-in-Publication Data
Muschal, Frank.
  Bio-fuels / by Frank Muschal.
    p. cm. — (Power up!)
  Includes index.
    ISBN-13: 978-1-60279-045-2 (lib. bdg.)   978-1-60279-094-0 (pbk.)
    ISBN-10: 1-60279-045-0 (lib. bdg.)   1-60279-094-9 (pbk.)
  1. Biomass energy—Juvenile literature. I. Title. II. Series.
  TP339.M87 2008
  662'.88—dc22   2007005618

Cherry Lake Publishing would like to acknowledge the work of
The Partnership for 21st Century Skills.
Please visit www.21stcenturyskills.org *for more information.*

TABLE OF CONTENTS

CHAPTER ONE

Bio-fuels

Corn grows well in much of the United States, but especially in states such as Iowa and Illinois.

Most Americans agree that we need new sources of energy. Even though

the U.S. has some petroleum resources, we don't have enough for our

needs. Much of the petroleum we use comes from other countries, and it's getting expensive. We do have lots of coal, but burning it can cause lots of air pollution.

Fortunately, other energy sources are being studied. Solar power, wind power, and tidal power are some of them. However, bio-fuels are the most promising.

Bio-fuel is any fuel produced from organic matter. When organic matter is used in the production of this fuel, it is called biomass. It can be made from crops that are widely grown in the United States. They include corn and soybeans. It can also be made from other crops such as sugar cane. Biomass can also come from processed animal fats, solid waste, and many industrial wastes.

Learning & Innovation Skills

Creating energy from animal waste is not a new idea. In the 1800s, people on the Great Plains often used buffalo chips (manure) as a cooking fuel. The joke was that steaks cooked over buffalo chips required no pepper. Do you already use bio-fuels at your house? *Hint*: If you have a fireplace, what do you burn in it?

Bio-fuels get their energy from the sun. So did the coal, petroleum, and natural gas that Americans use in huge amounts every day. However, coal, petroleum, and natural gas take millions of years to be created. Some bio-fuels can be made in less than a year. There are three major types of bio-fuel: **bio-diesel, bio-methane,** and **ethanol**. Each type has its own process and ingredients.

CHAPTER TWO

Bio-diesel

Many of America's favorite foods contain large amounts of fats and oils.

Bio-diesel is made chiefly from animal fats and vegetable oils. Even

recycled cooking oil can be used to make bio-diesel. The oils and fats are

combined with alcohol and a catalyst to produce bio-diesel.

When cars use this fuel, their exhaust often has a pleasant smell, similar to food that is cooking. That's a big improvement over the exhaust of cars running on petroleum-based fuels. Of course, people near a bio-diesel car might get hungry from the aroma!

Diesel engines are good for heavy-duty jobs like pulling trains and propelling ocean liners, and bio-diesel can be used in these engines. The bio-diesel can be as little as 5 percent or as much as 100 percent of the total fuel. The more bio-diesel that is in the blend, the more efficiently the engines will run. However, they do need some changes to run on 100 percent bio-diesel fuel. Engines running on lower percentages of bio-diesel do not.

Bio-diesel fuel creates less air pollution than petroleum products. It also cleans and lubricates the moving parts of diesel engines. Plus, bio-diesel is more efficient to produce. It takes one unit of energy to make 3.2 units of bio-diesel energy. It takes more than one unit of energy to produce one unit of petroleum-based diesel energy. So, why don't more vehicles use bio-diesel fuels? Because petroleum-based diesel is still cheaper to produce.

Bio-diesel fuel pumps are becoming more common at gas stations across America.

CHAPTER THREE

ETHANOL

*Henry Ford introduced his wildly popular Model T in 1908, and
that "sealed the deal" for gasoline for the twentieth century.*

When Henry Ford first developed his famous Model T automobile, he planned to make it run on a bio-fuel called ethanol. At that time, however, the petroleum industry was beginning to make inexpensive gasoline. Because gasoline was cheaper, Ford decided to use a gasoline engine in his Model T. The Model T was wildly successful, eventually selling 15 million cars. Soon all other automobiles used gasoline-burning engines, too.

The process for producing ethanol is similar to that for producing alcoholic beverages. First, the biomass is converted to sugar. Then the sugar is fermented into alcohol. Ethanol has an alcohol

Learning & Innovation Skills

In 2006, all the race cars in the Indianapolis 500 used fuel with ten percent ethanol. Reportedly, the cars ran faster and got better mileage than they did with "regular" fuel. Why do you think the move to fuels other than petroleum has been so slow?

21st Century Content

In addition to the U.S., other world regions are producing materials for or planning uses of bio-fuels. Brazil, Southeast Asia, and other sites are converting crops into bio-fuel. The European Union has set a goal that by 2010 each member should achieve at least 5.75 percent of all energy from bio-fuel.

content of 95 percent, while most alcoholic beverages are less than 50 percent alcohol. But don't try drinking ethanol! It's definitely for engines, not people.

Ethanol is produced chiefly from the leftover stalks of wheat and corn. Ethanol can also be produced from the nonedible portions of foods, such as tomato vines, grapefruit rinds, orange peels, and peach pits. The major drawback of these sources is transporting the biomass to processing plants. However, our landfills are rapidly reaching their capacity. Construction of nearby plants could provide a partial solution to two environmental challenges that we face today.

Another source for ethanol is switchgrass. For centuries, it covered much of America's Great Plains. It grew so tall, thick, and hardy that children sometimes got lost in it. Then in the 1800s, homesteaders plowed it under so they could plant corn, wheat, and other crops. Now it is being grown again. It can produce one or even two crops a year for ten years before it needs to be replanted.

Switchgrass is native to North America and is naturally resistant to many plant diseases and pests.

A lot of plastic is also made from petroleum. What are the factors you need to consider when buying a product? Is the environment on your list? Why or why not?

Switchgrass has many advantages. It doesn't reduce soil fertility as much as other crops. Its deep penetrating roots help prevent soil erosion. Also, because switchgrass grows so quickly, it stores more solar energy and removes more bad carbon dioxide from the air than do other crops. Finally, a big advantage of switchgrass is the byproducts produced by processing it into ethanol. These can be used to make fertilizers, solvents, and plastics.

CHAPTER FOUR

BIO-METHANE

Studies of ice from deep under Antarctica have shown that the Earth is warmer now than any time in the past 650,000 years.

Methane is both good and bad. It is a greenhouse gas, which is bad.

But it is also a necessary part of our atmosphere. Methane helps absorb

dangerous infrared rays. It also heats the surface of the Earth so we can live here. However, methane and other greenhouse gases are becoming a problem.

Earth's climate is warmer now than it has been for thousands of years. Scientists are looking for ways to reduce methane and other greenhouse gases.

Methane occurs naturally. It makes up a large proportion of natural gas. Some volcanoes belch out methane. Permafrost, which covers about 25 percent of the Earth's surface, also contains methane. It is released when the permafrost melts. Swamps, marshes, and other bodies of shallow, standing water generate methane, too.

*Fermented cow manure produces methane
that farmers can use to generate electricity.*

Some animals produce large amounts of methane. Termites are a major

source. Some estimates say that termites create 25 percent of all methane.

Cows produce methane when they belch.

Human activity creates methane. Our cars and factories generate a lot of methane, but they are only part of the problem. Even the cardboard boxes and paper wrappers that our food comes in generate methane as they **decompose**.

Spontaneous fires can break out in landfills when methane builds up below the surface. Usually the fires begin as smoldering patches below ground. They burst into flame when the surface layer is disturbed. The sudden contact with oxygen causes the flames.

Growing rice requires large amounts of water and takes from 100 to 120 days for a single crop.

The food we eat makes methane. For example, rice is an important

food for more than half the world's population. Most of it is grown

underwater in paddies, and they generate great quantities of methane.

The food we don't eat makes methane, too. Think of banana peels, coffee grounds, and bread crusts. They release methane into the air as they break down. Scientists estimate that the amount of methane in our atmosphere has grown by 140 percent in the past 250 years.

Making Methane Work for Us

So, a lot of methane is being released into the atmosphere. However, it's not methane that we can easily use for our energy needs. For example, how could we collect a cow's belches?

We *can* collect and use some methane, however. One way is through treating solid human waste in sewage plants. The sewage is processed in oxygen-free tanks. As it

breaks down, methane is released. Then this bio-methane can be collected

and used as fuel.

Modern sewage plants process wastewater from homes, schools,
factories, offices, restaurants, hotels, and elsewhere.

Learning & Innovation Skills

In 1984, methane built up in some New York sewers. They exploded and shattered windows in 12 buildings. Three vehicles were badly damaged, and dozens of manhole covers blew off. What does this explosion show about the energy that methane contains?

Farm animals produce methane, but they also produce a lot of manure. Today, some plants collect the manure and process it into bio-methane. Other farm biomass can be used to produce bio-methane, too. For example, the edible part of rice is just the small grains, and they don't burn very well. However, the dried stalks and leaves are a different matter. Researchers and farmers in Texas are now looking for efficient ways to turn these "leftovers" into bio-methane.

Every year, Americans throw away about 72 million tons (65 million metric tons) of paper trash and 32 million tons (29 million metric tons) of yard waste.

Many American cities now recycle newspaper,
cans, glass jars, and some types of plastic.

These, along with food scraps, make up about 65 percent of all trash. And all three can be processed into bio-methane! That's why many American cities and towns now have recycling programs. Collecting these products separately allows communities to keep them out of overflowing landfills. It also allows these products to become new sources of energy.

We can do little about much of the methane that goes into the air. All living creatures must eat, and eating eventually causes methane. However,

Life & Career Skills

Many people believe recycling is everyone's responsibility. Many locales now require the recycling of certain items. Some day items that could yield methane could be high on the lists.

we can turn some of the methane we create into bio-methane to help our energy needs. Pigs and cows won't mind if we collect their manure and use it to heat the barn in winter. Turning those unwanted catalogs and other mail into power for your computer will be a good thing, too.

Let's not fool ourselves. Burning bio-fuels puts methane into the air, too. The difference is that the methane from bio-fuels would go into the atmosphere anyway as part of the natural decaying and digesting processes. Burning coal, natural gas, and petroleum products adds methane to the atmosphere that has been locked underground for millions of years. Those unlocked gases, plus the gases from natural

organic decay, are creating the greenhouse effect that has scientists worried.

The United States has large reserves of coal, but burning it can cause large amounts of air pollution, too.

CHAPTER FIVE

INTO THE FUTURE

Sugar cane for ethanol grows well in Brazil as well as in the U.S. states of Florida, Louisiana, and Hawaii.

Think that bio-fuel can't replace gasoline? Think again. Brazil and

Sweden are proving that it can.

Sweden is already running cars, buses, and even trains on bio-methane. The nation also has more than 7,000 cars that can run on either gasoline or ethanol. To keep these cars running, there are 320 ethanol stations scattered across the country. Some of Sweden's ethanol is produced from logging waste.

Brazil is leading the worldwide bio-fuels movement. For more than 30 years, the nation has been working to solve its energy needs with homegrown products rather than imported oil. Today, Brazil is the world's largest producer of ethanol. Brazil produces so much ethanol that it exports some to Europe. All of this ethanol is made from sugar cane,

21st Century Content

The British government has estimated that burning ethanol produces 65 percent *less* greenhouse gas than burning regular gasoline does.

*Destroying the rainforests in Brazil and elsewhere
may someday affect the air we all breathe.*

which grows well there. Brazil currently produces more than 15 billion

liters of ethanol per year. Millions of Brazilian cars run on it.

The bad side is that Brazil has been destroying its rainforest to make

room for sugar cane, and Brazil's rainforest makes up about 40 percent of

the world's total. This rainforest is the planet's lungs. It is key to keeping the atmosphere healthy all over the planet because the trees help clean pollution out of the air. Plus, the leftover tree waste is a problem. Termites love it, and we all know that termites produce a lot of methane!

Why should Americans want bio-fuels? There are several reasons. One is that we don't have enough petroleum in our country to meet our needs. However, we can grow and create bio-fuels ourselves. A second reason deals with waste. Making bio-methane can help us put our trash to good use. A final reason is the air we breathe. Using bio-fuels can help us keep pollution out of the atmosphere. Altogether, bio-fuels are good for us and our planet.

Glossary

bio-diesel (BAHY-oh DEE-suhl) fuel for diesel engines produced from crops such as corn, wheat, etc.

bio-fuels (BAHY-oh FYOO-uhlz) types of fuels made from crops, trash, etc.

biomass (BAHY-oh-mas) large amount of material that will be used to make bio-fuel

bio-methane (BAHY-oh METH-eyn) specific type of methane fuel made from bio-fuels

byproducts (bahy-PROD-uhkts) products that occur incidentally during the purposeful manufacture of another product

capacity (kuh-PAS-i-tee) maximum amount that a container can hold

catalyst (KAT-l-ist) substance that speeds up a chemical reaction between other substances without being changed itself

decompose (dee-kuhm-POHZ) to break down from a complex organism into its more basic forms

erosion (i-ROH-zhuhn) washing away of topsoil by moving water

ethanol (ETH-uh-nawl) colorless, flammable liquid that can be used as a bio-fuel

fermented (fer-MENT-ed) chemically changed by microorganisms

permafrost (PUR-muh-frawst) permanently frozen soil that covers about 85 percent of Alaska and more than half of Canada and Russia

petroleum (puh-TROH-lee-uhm) oil below the Earth's crust that can be refined into gasoline and other products

recycling programs (ree-SAHY-kuhl-ng PROH-grams) official plans to collect and reuse certain types of trash

spontaneous (spon-TEY-nee-uhs) occurring without any apparent outside cause

ADDITIONAL RESOURCES

Books

Gifford, Clive. *How the Future Began: Machines.*
New York: Kingfisher, 2000.

Hayhurst, Chris. *Biofuel—Power of the Future:*
New Ways of Turning Organic Matter into Energy.
New York: Rosen Publishing Group, 2003.

Petersen, Christine. *Alternative Energy (True Books).*
New York: Children's Press, 2004.

Povey, Karen D. *Biofuels (Our Environment).*
San Diego: KidHaven Press, 2006.

Roa, Michael L. *Environmental Science Activities Kit:*
Ready-To-Use Lessons, Labs and Worksheets for Grades 7–12.
West Nyack, NY: Center for Applied Research in Education,
Jossey-Bass Press, 1993.

Other Media

To learn more about bio-diesel, see *http://www.eia.doe.*
gov/kids/energyfacts/sources/renewable/biodiesel.html

To find out about how natural gas and oil are produced,
go to *http://www.adventuresinenergy.org/*

INDEX

ABOUT THE AUTHOR

Frank Muschal lives in Chicago with his elderly cat, Agatha. ("She's older than laptops and cell phones, but I'm older than TV.") He's been writing and editing for textbook publishers for thirty years and has no guilt feelings about tormenting students all that time. Besides writing, Frank keeps busy playing tennis, riding horses, and fumbling around on his guitar. "I'm no rock star," he says. "I just want to make me more interesting to myself."